How to Bigger

Aim Higher,
Get More Motivated,
and Accomplish Big Things

By Martin Meadows

Download another Book for Free

I want to thank you for buying my book and offer you another book (just as long and valuable as this book), *Grit: How to Keep Going When You Want to Give Up*, completely free.

Click the link below to receive it:

http://www.profoundselfimprovement.com/thinkbigger

In *Grit*, I'll share with you how exactly to stick to your goals according to peak performers and science.

In addition to getting *Grit*, you'll also have an opportunity to get my new books for free, enter giveaways and receive other valuable emails from me.

Again, here's the link to sign up:

http://www.profoundselfimprovement.com/thinkbigger

Table of Contents

Download another Book for Free 2

Table of Contents 3

Prologue 5

Chapter 1: What Makes You Ambitious? 8

Chapter 2: What's Your Why (or Who)? 21

Chapter 3: Chimp vs. Human – How Your Primal Brain Prevents You from Thinking Bigger 36

Chapter 4: Competitiveness and Collaboration Drive Ambition 48

Chapter 5: The Art of Focus 60

Chapter 6: How to Achieve the Impossible 74

Chapter 7: The Dangers of Being Overly Ambitious (and How to Avoid Them) 86

Epilogue 94

Appendix A: Books You Need to Read 97

Download another Book for Free 102

Could You Help? 103

About Martin Meadows 104

If you think you are beaten, you are
If you think you dare not, you don't,
If you like to win, but you think you can't
It is almost certain you won't.

If you think you'll lose, you're lost
For out of the world we find,
Success begins with a fellow's will
It's all in the state of mind.

If you think you are outclassed, you are
You've got to think high to rise,
You've got to be sure of yourself before
You can ever win a prize.

Life's battles don't always go
To the stronger or faster man,
But soon or late the man who wins
Is the man WHO THINKS HE CAN!

"Thinking" by Walter D. Wintle

Prologue

Have you ever wondered what separates people who think bigger from people who set their bar low? What makes one person accept low standards and another person constantly raise them?

Why one person strives to build an international organization affecting the lives of millions of people, while another person is content working her entire life as a clerk? (Not that there's anything wrong with being a clerk!)

Why does one person challenge herself to run marathons, train her body and get fitter, while another is happy living a sedentary, unhealthy lifestyle?

What drives a person who's optimizing every single aspect of her life and what causes another person to maintain the status quo?

You can say, "Well, the answer is simple enough – one person is ambitious, while the other one is not." But what exactly causes it? And most importantly – how do you become more ambitious and think bigger? Is it something you're born with and can't change it, or is it something over which you have control?

I found this topic so fascinating I decided to find out the answer for myself and write a book about it. This book is the result of my research about people who think big and the science of being more ambitious.

Before we move on to the first chapter, there are several things I need to clarify to make sure we're on the same page.

First and foremost, while many examples in this book come from billionaires and successful entrepreneurs, this book isn't about how to become one (though it can probably help you). If you're looking for a book on how to become rich, this book is not for you. I researched the mindset behind thinking big, not the business processes. This book is not necessarily for people who are or want to be entrepreneurs.

The goal of this book is to help you learn how to find motivation to become the best version of you. It doesn't matter if your idea of big thinking is running a billion-dollar company or being a respectable member of your community. The objective is to understand how to get yourself fired up to constantly raise your standards.

Secondly, if you decided to read this book, I assume there's already some motivation to change inside you – even if it's tiny and you struggle with procrastination. Only you can tell if it's really there or if you're content with what you have now. This book won't magically make you ambitious. It can only help you find out how to improve your motivation and think bigger.

Last but not least, there's nothing wrong with not dreaming big. The key to a happy life is fulfillment. If you find fulfillment in a simple, unchallenging life, there's absolutely nothing wrong with it. However, you're probably not my target reader, and the topics I'll cover in this book won't appeal to you.

I wrote this book to increase my motivation, teach myself how to think bigger and learn how to raise my standards. I hope the answer I found will help you as much as it has helped me.

Chapter 1: What Makes You Ambitious?

There's a common belief that genes and upbringing have a huge influence on whether someone is ambitious or not. Yet, it isn't that simple.

Children of billionaires can either follow their parents' tracks and build another successful billion-dollar company, or the cozy life can turn them into vain and unproductive people. Children born in poor families can "inherit" learned helplessness and stay poor just like their parents. Or their hunger for success will drive them to improve their situation.

If there's one thing we can say about upbringing and ambitions, it's that there's no clear correlation between your background and what you're going to achieve in life.

Some anthropologists[i] suggest that members of the upper middle class are most driven to achievement. Unlike the poor, they're not struggling to get by. And unlike the rich, they still feel hunger to achieve more.

However, it still doesn't explain why many wealthy people still strive for more and why some people coming from a poor background overcome their unfavorable circumstances. There are several reasons we'll investigate in this chapter. Since we can't change our background and upbringing, we'll focus only on the causes we can directly control.

Examples around You

Let's start with the most obvious cause – social modeling.

According to the social learning theory, learning takes place in a social context. You can adapt new behaviors purely through observation[ii]. If you have ever changed one of your behaviors because you observed it in your friends (say, you started wearing collared shirts on a daily basis because that's how your friends dress), it's social modeling at work.

Everything that surrounds you on a daily basis has an influence on you. Rolf Dobelli, bestselling author of *The Art of Thinking Clearly*, wrote an essay about the influence of news on your life[iii]. He writes that news triggers your limbic system, almost as if you were constantly on the lookout for threats. This heightened state of awareness leads to chronic stress, a deregulated immune system, fear, and aggression.

And that's just the result of watching or reading news. People who surround you have a much stronger impact on your behavior, including whether you're ambitious or avoid any challenges.

Fortunately, we can choose what examples we allow in our lives.

The first and most easily accessible source of the right examples is books. Many successful people (Peter Diamandis, Tony Robbins, and Tim Ferriss, to name a few[iv]) credit books as the number one reason for their success in life.

One simple change – replacing news and mass media with books – can produce dramatic changes in your life. No matter what your ambition in life is, you can find books that will inspire you to work on your goals.

Direct, in-person influence of successful people is another source that can fire you up to achieve big things in your life. However, meeting successful people is not as easy as buying a book. Unless you live in the Silicon Valley or any other place populated with successful people you want to emulate, it takes much more work to find them.

Thankfully, the Internet makes it extremely easy to interact with such individuals. Although meeting these people in person will have a much more powerful impact on you, talking with them online is still a viable way to light the fire inside you.

Studies show[v] that observing people you view as similar to you improves your self-efficacy (the strength of the belief in your abilities, which I discussed in my book *Confidence: How to Overcome Your Limiting Beliefs and Achieve Your Goals*) more than watching people with whom you don't share as much. In other words, you'll get more fired up by watching people similar to you succeed than by watching people who are much more skilled than you (please note it doesn't mean you'll learn more from them – it's best to emulate the most successful people).

I'm a huge fan of online communities like forums, membership sites and groups on social media sites. Since they are populated by people at all levels of competence, you can easily find people just a little better than you who will motivate you to raise your standards.

It's easier to relate to and get motivated by an entrepreneur who has gone from $1000 per month to $5000 per month in a span of six months than from a billionaire who has launched yet another million-dollar business.

Watching a person who successfully loses fifty pounds and changes her life is more inspirational than listening to a fitness coach with a perfect body.

Surrounding yourself with empowering books and people on a daily basis will put you into a positive state that will inspire you to raise your standards. Please keep in mind it's a process of conditioning, and it's never-ending.

Stay Away from Negativity

Since we tend to process negative information more thoroughly than good feedback[vi], it's crucial to reduce or eliminate negative stimuli from our lives.

People who discourage you from setting big goals decrease your motivation more effectively than empowering people increase it. If you have ever shared a big goal with someone and she told you, "Get real, you'll never achieve it," you probably understand how much more destructive it is than words of encouragement.

It's not always possible to eliminate toxic relationships from your life, but the less time you spend with these people, the better it will be for both your mental health and personal success.

Be aware of your surroundings and try to replace the bad influence with positive feedback. If you find it extremely hard to distance yourself from the negativity, consider moving to a different place and starting anew.

Your Energy and a Sense of Urgency

There are two kinds of ambitious people – people who have big goals and act on them, and people who say "one day I'll do X," but never do it. The difference between these two kinds of people is, among others, their level of energy and urgency.

British billionaire Richard Branson, when asked about his secret of productivity, gave a surprisingly simple answer: "Work out.[vii]" It's his physical wellness that keeps his brain sharp and his body ready to constantly travel all over the world, build new industry-changing businesses and solve some of the world's biggest problems.

Perhaps it sounds cliché, but physical wellbeing is indeed one of the keys to success. If you don't demand much from your body, how much more will you demand from yourself in other areas of your life? If your body doesn't work on the highest level, how are you supposed to work on the big goals?

The second difference between "someday" people and people who take action right away is their sense of urgency. What drives them to achieve more is their perception of time – life is short, and they want to make the most out of it. Hence, they set big goals. They don't have time to work on small thinking, because it's only the bold ideas that will lead to exponential results.

There is also another reason why ambitious action-takers are so driven to do everything right now instead of waiting for the right time – we'll discuss it in more detail in the second chapter.

Your Needs

Poor people who struggle to get by can't afford the luxury of high ambitions. It's hard to think big when you're not sure if you can pay the bills or afford to buy food this month. The constant fight to stay afloat robs you of the energy to think in the long term.

Maslow's hierarchy of needs suggests that self-actualization (the drive to achieve your full potential) and self-transcendence (giving yourself to higher goals like spirituality or altruism) can only happen if all other, lower needs (food, shelter, security, a sense of belongingness, etc.) are satisfied first.

For reference, here's Maslow's hierarchy of needs in a graphic form:

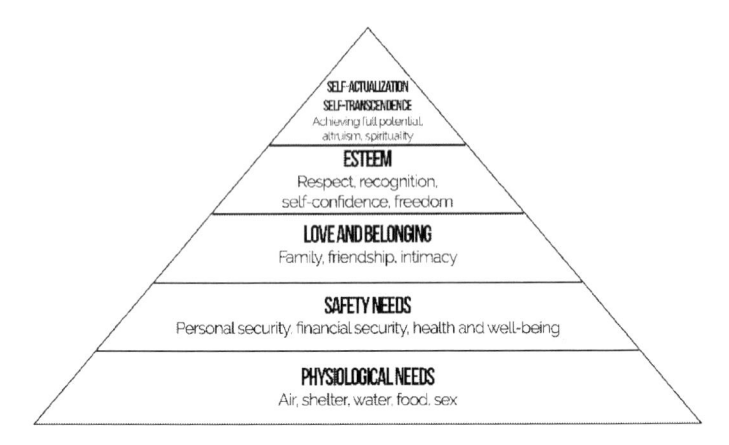

SELF-ACTUALIZATION
SELF-TRANSCENDENCE
Achieving full potential, altruism, spirituality

ESTEEM
Respect, recognition, self-confidence, freedom

LOVE AND BELONGING
Family, friendship, intimacy

SAFETY NEEDS
Personal security, financial security, health and well-being

PHYSIOLOGICAL NEEDS
Air, shelter, water, food, sex

If you want to achieve big things, but you can't motivate yourself to work on them, perhaps you're lacking one of the lower needs. If you're fortunate enough to read this book, we can eliminate the most basic needs like food, shelter, and safety.

There are two groups of needs that might block you from thinking big – a sense of belongingness and esteem.

The feeling of being loved – both sexually and non-sexually – is a basic need that is much more important than the quest to reach your full potential. If, on some level, you feel lonely, your first step toward becoming more ambitious could be working on this aspect of your life.

Please note I'm not qualified to give you psychological or psychotherapeutic advice. If you struggle with social anxiety, the feeling of being unloved or depression due to a lack of intimacy, speak with a trained psychologist or psychiatrist.

Esteem is the second need that, if unmet, will overpower your need for self-actualization. For years, I was an extremely shy person. My crippling shyness cast a shadow on my life and blocked me from realizing my full potential. It was only when I overcame shyness that I observed dramatic changes in other areas of my life and could focus on the bigger goals.

Low self-esteem – the feeling that you're worse than other people – will lead you to self-sabotage. Until you become more confident of your self-worth, achieving bold goals will be too big of a challenge to you, as you will underestimate your abilities.

If you feel inferior to others or you're extremely shy, solving these problems is more important than learning how to become more ambitious. Shyness will stand in your way your entire life. Until you fix it, it won't be likely you'll achieve your big dreams. Take it from a person who was there and knows how poisoning it is.

WHAT MAKES YOU AMBITIOUS? QUICK RECAP

1. Things and people who surround you influence how ambitious you are. Reading books and surrounding yourself with other ambitious people are two of the most effective ways to light a fire in your belly.

2. Negative stimuli are more powerful at discouraging you than words of encouragement are at motivating you. Consequently, it's crucial to avoid or eliminate from your life people whose behaviors and opinions put you down.

3. Physical wellness is one of the keys of people who think big. If you don't have enough energy, you won't have enough motivation to put your plans into action. Demand from yourself the best – both physically and mentally.

4. A sense of urgency is necessary if you want to act on your goals now instead of "someday." Successful people don't have time for small thinking because they want to make the most out of their time on Earth.

5. You can't focus on achieving your full potential if you lack the more basic needs in your life such as a sense of belongingness and esteem. If you suffer from shyness, social anxiety, or depression, your plan of action should start with fixing these issues.

Chapter 2: What's Your Why (or Who)?

If you look at the most successful people, like Richard Branson or Tony Robbins, you'll quickly notice how fired up and passionate they are about their goals.

They exhibit bold thinking because they're after making the biggest impact.. But what is the source of this passion?

The answer is simple – they have a deep internal drive, a vision that directs all their actions. Without a powerful "why," big achievements are close to impossible. We all need strong internal motivation to act on our goals.

It sounds simple enough, but there's much more to it than just writing down that you want to be a millionaire or drive a Lamborghini.

Why Is Not about Money (and Other Superficial Things)

Various studies show that money is not the best motivator, especially after a certain level of income.

A well-known paper written by Daniel Kahneman and Angus Deaton[viii] suggests that emotional well-being rises until we make $75,000 per year. Beyond this number, there's no further improvement in life satisfaction. We can draw a conclusion that past $75,000 in annual income, money (and things it can buy) won't motivate you to think bigger, as it won't affect your well-being.

An analysis of over 200,000 U.S. public sector employees[ix] shows that intrinsic motives (passion, challenge, etc.) are three times more powerful than extrinsic motives (e.g. money). In other words, people who focus on the job they perform are more engaged in it (i.e. more driven) than people who focus on the money they make from it.

Another study on extrinsic and intrinsic motivators[x] shows that intrinsic motivation leads to better job performance than external motivators. You care more and get better results when there's a deeper reason for what you're doing than just money.

When you put too much focus on the money itself, you'll get less enjoyment from your job, which will negatively affect your well-being.

However, a study conducted on entrepreneurs[xi] suggests that it's the motive of making money and not the money itself that affects subjective well-being negatively.

When people want to make money because they want to keep up with the Joneses, have more power, show off, or overcome self-doubt, that's when their well-being is affected negatively. If you want to make money to help your parents, take care of your family, or help those in need, it won't affect your well-being negatively.

What does all of this research tells us?

First and foremost, if you want to become more driven to realize your full potential, don't focus on money as your sole motivation. Find a deeper reason why – your intrinsic motivation.

Intrinsic motivation is about enjoyment, fulfillment, or challenge – anything that comes from within you rather than the influences outside of you.

Richard Branson has powerful intrinsic motivation: "My interest in life comes from setting myself huge, apparently unachievable challenges and trying to rise above them.[xii]"

Secondly, if your goal is somehow related to a specific amount of money (e.g., you'd like to make enough money to buy a boat and sail around the world), break it down into emotions you're after.

You're not after the boat itself – you're after the thrill, the sun on your face, the calmness of the sea, the smell of the ocean in the morning, and pure enjoyment of the adventure. It's thinking about these things that will fire you up rather than thinking about the act of buying a boat or what kind of an interior your boat will have.

Last but not least, if you've been working on a certain goal only because you're motivated by an extrinsic reward (say, you want to show off in a

Lamborghini), reconsider your goal and change your motivator.

It Can Be Your "Who," Not Only "Why"

Your motivation can get even stronger when instead of thinking about something from which you'll benefit, it will be someone else (usually your significant other or a family member).

A paper[xiii] by professor and bestselling author of *Give and Take: A Revolutionary Approach to Success* Adam Grant suggests that the desire to help others (prosocial motivation) makes us go the extra mile and work even more effectively than if we had intrinsic motivation alone.

For this reason, finding your "who" (the person for whom you're striving to achieve a big goal) can be even better than finding your "why."

If you already have a vision that draws from intrinsic motivators, consider adding prosocial motivation. If you have a goal to build a million-dollar business to challenge yourself, find a reason why it's going to make a positive difference in the world and make it a part of your vision.

Elon Musk, cofounder of PayPal, founder of Tesla Motors and SpaceX, is a perfect example of a person driven by prosocial motivation. He said, "Going from PayPal, I thought well, what are some of the other problems that are likely to most affect the future of humanity? Not from the perspective, 'What's the best way to make money,' which is okay, but, it was really, 'What do I think is going to most affect the future of humanity.'[xiv]"

Write It Down

If you've been trying to motivate yourself to work on a certain goal, write down your vision. If you've written it properly (meaning: it fires you up so much you're restless), you should no longer struggle with procrastination.

When writing your vision, go into deep details of what you want to achieve. Describe not only the achievement itself, but also how it makes you feel and what kind of a person you've become while working on it. The more senses and perspectives the vision will contain, the more powerful it will be.

Here's an example of a weak sentence in a vision:

I own a multi-million dollar business that is the leader in the industry.

Here's an example of how you can fix it:

I own a multi-million dollar business that is known for the passion it brings to the market. It brings a smile to my face just to think about it. Whenever I speak with my employees and partners, I'm fired up and feel immense hunger to improve our products and make the lives of our clients even easier. There's nothing in the world I love doing more than speaking with our clients and learning from their feedback. The constant growth makes me a better person and positively affects the lives of my wife and children.

After writing the first draft of your vision, each time you read it again, the motivational effect will get weaker – until it mostly serves as a reminder of your goals with a slight motivational boost.

Here's where routines comes into play.

The Importance of a Morning Routine

Writing down your vision alone won't do much to change your long-term motivation. In order to fully benefit from this practice, you need to establish a morning routine to prepare you for the day ahead and remind you of your big goal.

In his interview with Tim Ferriss[xv], Tony Robbins explains how he primes himself for the day ahead and is ready to work on his goals even after two hours of sleep. After meditative practice, toughening up (cold exposure), and expressing gratitude, he spends the next 10 minutes thinking about his vision.

It's a habit he has been practicing for several decades. Looking at his accomplishments, I'd say it's working exquisitely well for him.

While you don't necessarily have to follow the exact same morning routine as Tony, thinking about your vision is a practice you shouldn't skip.

However, there's an important caveat – don't let the false sense of achievement coming from envisioning your goal make you lazy. Studies show[xvi] it's the visualization of the process that's more important than thinking about the event itself. For the best results, your vision should include the actions you need to take to achieve it and then the event to which it will lead.

I personally start each day with expressing gratitude (I think about three things I'm grateful for), meditation to clear my mind and start the day slowly, and foam rolling (a form of stretching to relax the muscles). When I'm in this more awake and relaxed state of mind, I re-read my vision and other documents describing my goals, helping me prepare for the day ahead.

Why the Proper Mindset Is Paramount to Thinking Bigger

The most important thing I've learned over the years of making changes in my personal and business life is the pivotal role of mindset in achievement. Many people think that if they just had X or Y, they would most certainly succeed. Sorry, buddy – that's not how it works. There's no going past the mindset part. If your head is filled with self-doubt, it will find a way to make you sabotage your efforts.

A cliché, misattributed[xvii] Henry Ford quote, "Whether you think you can, or you think you can't, you're right," is correct. There's no substitute for the certainty that you can achieve your goal. Your mind will either help you achieve your goal or sabotage you. It gives you exactly what you feed it. Give it self-doubt, and you'll get self-defeat. Give it empowering thoughts, and it will be your best pal.

By creating your vision, and most importantly, re-reading it every single day and visualizing the outcome, your mindset will shift and your physiology will reflect it. You'll get more energized to work, you'll increase your discipline, and you'll get more focused and fired up to keep going.

This is not just feel-good talk. It works better than any other success secret, if you only implement it in your life. I can't stress the importance of the mindset enough. Nothing matters without the proper conditioning of your mind.

For the best results, combine visualizing the outcome with an NLP technique called anchoring – associating an internal feeling with an external trigger.

Let's say your goal is to lose fifty pounds and start running marathons. You visualize the process and the outcome, and your mind slowly fills up with positive emotions associated with achieving this goal. You feel energized, pumped up to put on your shoes and go running, ready to do whatever it takes to make your vision come true.

At the peak of this emotion, perform a certain gesture you'd like to associate with this state. For instance, it can be squeezing your knuckle or grabbing your wrist. The key here is to perform the exact same gesture each time you feel this specific state – it will reinforce your anchor. Once you repeat this process enough times (over the span of several days or weeks), you'll be able to access this resourceful state at will.

You can perform a similar process for any other emotion you'd like to re-access with a specific trigger – relaxation, determination, creativity, joy, and so on.

If you were to remember just one thing from this book, it's this short subchapter – every single day, develop more certainty in your abilities to succeed.

Put yourself in a prime state by visualizing and anchoring.

Cultivate Rituals

Having a vision and a morning routine are two keys to optimizing your life and starting each day on the right note. However, nothing will happen if you don't actually take action toward achieving your goals. Here's where rituals make all the difference.

Many people are focused on the event, while it's the process that leads to success. Weight loss pills, overnight millionaire programs, and short-term diets are all targeted at people who believe change can happen with a single event. Your rituals make you the person you are. No lasting change can happen in your life unless you change them first.

When I was an overweight person, my rituals were completely different than they are now that I'm a fit and lean individual. I ate mostly junk food and didn't exercise a lot. I still remember saying, "I don't care if it's healthy. All I care about is if it's tasty."

No surprise that I was 30 pounds overweight. I'm sure that if somebody took away all my excess weight, I would regain it all (and then some) in a few months. There's no way to make a permanent change to your body if you don't change your mindset.

When I changed my rituals – by applying permanent changes to my diet and incorporating exercise in my daily routine – I started losing weight, and never regained it. Today, my routines are the total opposite of who I was back then.

What kind of rituals do you have in your life and how do they affect your growth? Do they hinder it or empower you? If they don't serve you, change them. Charles Duhigg's book *The Power of Habit*[xviii] will teach you how to change your habits and incorporate new rituals.

WHAT'S YOUR WHY (OR WHO)? QUICK RECAP

1. Big achievements are impossible without strong, internal motivation.

2. Intrinsic motivators like fulfillment, enjoyment, and contribution are much more powerful than extrinsic motivators like money, fame or power. If you want to get fired up to work on your goals, discover a reason that comes from within you – not the pursuit of status or money.

3. If your goal can't be achieved without making a lot of money, tie it to the emotions you'll get from your purchase, and not the purchase itself.

4. Prosocial motivation (the desire to help others) is a more powerful motivator than intrinsic motivation. Consider adding a "who" to your "why."

5. When writing down your vision, make it as detailed as possible by using different senses and perspectives. It has to be so good that you can't wait to act on your goals.

6. The purpose of having a written vision is to make it easier to think about it every single morning.

The way you wake up will affect your entire day, so make it count and develop your own empowering morning routine.

7. Your mindset is paramount to success. If you don't have the proper mindset, you won't achieve your goals. Empower yourself by visualizing your outcome and anchoring positive states.

8. Your life is the sum of your rituals. Successful people have completely different rituals than complacent individuals. Change your rituals to change your life.

Chapter 3: Chimp vs. Human – How Your Primal Brain Prevents You from Thinking Bigger

Life would be easy if all we had to do to achieve our goals was to come up with a vision, think about it every single morning and act on it. However, it's not that simple. We often get in the way of our goals. Neuroscience shows that there are several parts of our brain that affect our decision making process.

In his book *The Chimp Paradox*,[xix] sports psychiatrist Steve Peters simplifies a human brain to three main parts – the chimp (the most primal, emotional part of the brain), the human (the rational side of the brain) and the computer (the part governed by the chimp and the human, responsible for automatic behavior). These three parts have a huge influence on your decision making process.

What Your Chimp Loves the Most

The side that stands in your way when you want to achieve big goals is the chimp, the primal part of the brain that makes decisions based on emotions. One of the things your chimp loves the most is safety.

It sounds weird to talk about you like two different persons, but that's exactly what we are. If you want to change your life, you need to understand how these two sides of your brain affect you.

The chimp is constantly on the lookout for new dangers. The more vulnerable it feels, the more paranoid it becomes. Since the chimp doesn't operate rationally, it quickly jumps to conclusions and thinks in black and white.

Next to reproduction, the second most important objective of the chimp is self-survival. It's for this reason that it often sabotages us and prevents us from working on the big goals – it perceives challenges as dangers.

Starting a business can be scary. Your chimp will consider it a danger and try to keep you away from acting on this goal. Whenever you catch yourself thinking, "I feel it's too dangerous," it's probably your chimp at work.

This primal part of your brain doesn't like any changes that require effort. It loves comfort. Even waking up earlier or losing weight, both of which can tremendously benefit you in the long term, will be considered by your chimp as threats. Discomfort is not your chimp's friend, even if the human part of your brain knows how transformational short-term discomfort can be.

If you want to reduce the negative influence of the chimp on your decision making process, you need to understand how to calm it down.

Number One Technique to Calm down Your Chimp

Since your chimp is so dependent on its emotions, the primary way to manage it is to let yourself feel the emotions, acknowledge them and reason with them. We often keep the emotions boxed in and don't voice them, and thus we're never able to correctly identify them and deal with them.

Peters writes in his book that whenever thoughts such as "But I feel" or "I don't feel like" pop up in your mind, it's usually your chimp – not your human "you."

Many choices in our lives are unpleasant in the short term, but more than worthy in the long term. A 30-minute dental visit isn't on anyone's list of fun things to do, but the short-term pain is worth it – it helps us prevent long-term excruciating pain, worsened health, and a scary smile.

You can calm your chimp down by speaking to it logically and explaining what will happen if you try to avoid the short-term discomfort.

Let's say you want to start a business, but a fear of failure prevents you from doing it. What is the underlying emotion? Are you afraid of failure because people will laugh at you? Is it because you're afraid you'll lose self-confidence? Or perhaps you're afraid you'll lose financial security?

Whatever the deep reason is, until you discover it, you won't be able to manage your primal part of the brain and stop worrying. Once you voice all these emotions, you'll be able to address them one by one to put an end to self-sabotage.

Reasoning with the logical part of your brain will help you reduce the emotion that causes fear and prevents you from taking action. While performing this practice just once isn't likely to produce permanent results, repeating it several times should be enough to handle it.

Here's an example from my personal life. For a long time, I was afraid to launch any business that required more than a small amount of money to start. My reasoning was that the risk was too high. I was afraid of losing money, so I would pass on every business opportunity that required a bigger investment, even if there was a high chance of success.

Once I acknowledged this fear, I could manage it by reasoning.

Would starting a business requiring a higher investment ruin me financially? It would, but only if I made a stupid decision and invested all I had. If I set aside enough savings, my fear wouldn't be so crippling.

Was it 100% certain I would lose the money? It wasn't. In most cases, it's possible to at least break even or lose perhaps 50% of the invested money, but not 100%. By making a list of possible outcomes and actions I could take to reduce my losses (say, closing a business if I lose more than 50% of the initial investment), I could once again reduce my fear.

Reward the Chimp

Another technique you can use to reduce the negative influence of your primal part of the brain is to promise yourself a reward after doing something that the chimp considers threatening or uncomfortable.

Let's say you want to start waking up early, as you believe it will help you improve your productivity and accomplish your big goals. The chimp obviously doesn't feel like doing it – it's a change of the routine, and painful at that.

However, if you promise it a reward – say, a big cup of coffee or tea, it will help you get up. It's all about manipulating your emotions and coming up with short-term rewards that will recoup the pain of the short-term uncomfortable task. It also works because you'll start associating the painful act with something pleasurable.

You can also use the exact opposite of a reward – threaten your chimp with something worse if you don't perform a given action. When not making the change will be associated with pain, you'll be more motivated to make it.

Let's continue the example of waking up early. The primal part of the brain finds this change threatening, so instead of helping you get up it will tell you to nap for just a while longer. However, if you threaten it with a worse danger (say, you'll have to pay your friend $50 if you don't report to him by 6:15 AM), the chimp will want to minimize the pain and help you get up.

Replace Emotional Thinking with Routines

In addition to the human, rational side of the brain and the primal, emotional side of the brain, we possess a part of the brain that is responsible for automated behaviors – the computer. Both the chimp and the human can influence this part of the brain. That's how enabling and limiting beliefs come to life.

Let's say that you start a business and lose money you've invested in it. The chimp, thinking in black and white and always putting its survival as the priority, will put an instruction (a limiting belief) forth that starting a business is associated with losing money. The human, on the other hand, can put an instruction forth that business requires investment, and it takes several tries to get it right. If your chimp wins, you'll be scared to start another venture.

The good news is that you can identify your current disabling beliefs that prevent you from realizing your full potential. Just note down your beliefs and ask yourself if they serve your goals. If not, they're limiting. The process of eliminating negative beliefs and reinforcing the enabling ones is covered in Tony Robbins' books *Unlimited Power*[xx] and *Awaken the Giant Within*[xxi]. You owe it to yourself to read these books.

Below the layer of automated behaviors lies your personal philosophy – your most important values and truths that are unbendable. These core rules will guide your life and either help you achieve your goals or hinder your growth.

Consider writing down your personal philosophy. You can do it by making a list of your most important truths in life that you're going to follow no matter what.

Here are a few of my own truths that guide my behavior in life:

1. I never give up on anything that's important to me.

2. I don't care what anyone thinks about me. The only approval I need is my own.

3. Time is my most important asset. I always focus on achieving more with less.

4. I'm always honest. Lying is for cowards.

5. I always think carefully before making any promises because I always keep my word.

6. Growth happens outside comfort zone. Security leads to mediocrity.

7. I refuse an ordinary approach because I want to live an extraordinary life.

8. Nothing is impossible for a man who refuses to listen to reason.

9. Abundance is all around me. Scarcity is the mindset of the poor.

10. If it's not fun, I don't do it. If I have to, I find a way to delegate it.

These simple statements guide my life decisions and make it easier to deal with self-sabotage. You don't struggle with making a decision about giving up if you have a clear rule that states when you can't give up.

I strongly suggest re-reading your rules along with re-reading your vision. If you know them by heart, many decisions in your life will be much easier to take – including decisions that can help you achieve big goals.

CHIMP VS. HUMAN – HOW YOUR PRIMAL BRAIN PREVENTS YOU FROM THINKING BIGGER: QUICK RECAP

1. There are three parts of the brain: the chimp (the most primal, emotional part of the brain), the human (the rational side of the brain) and the computer (the part governed by the chimp and the human, responsible for automatic behavior).

2. The chimp loves security. It will prevent you from setting and working on big goals because it will feel threatened by them. The primal part of your brain puts self-survival as the most important thing (right after reproduction).

3. The most effective way to manage your chimp is to let yourself feel the emotions it feels, acknowledge them and reason with them by using the logical part of your brain.

4. Rewarding yourself or threatening yourself with a danger bigger than the short-term pain will help you motivate yourself to work on your goals. It's

all about associating the painful changes with pleasure and maintaining status quo with pain.

5. Replace emotional thinking with routines that empower you. Both the chimp and the human can put the instructions in your computer, but it's usually the human who puts in the enabling beliefs that can change your life for the better.

6. Write down your personal philosophy – the core values and truths that guide your life. They will make it easier to make the right, empowering decision.

Chapter 4: Competitiveness and Collaboration Drive Ambition

Humans have a competitive nature that you can use to your benefit to think bigger. However, there are two types of competitiveness. The first is positive and productive, which motivates you to strive for more, but not at the expense of others. The second is hypercompetitiveness, which is a "winning isn't everything; it's the only thing" type of thinking.

Healthy competitiveness (or rather, the effects of competition, which we'll discuss in a second) can inspire you to start working on your objectives, help you set bigger goals, and achieve more than you believe you can. Sounds interesting in theory, but how does it affect your real-world performance and how can you use it to motivate yourself? Let's dig deeper.

It's Not Competition in Itself that Improves Your Performance

A meta-analysis on competition and performance[xxii] showed that there was no relation between competing and results. However, when scientists dug deeper and conducted an additional meta-analysis and three new empirical studies, they found there are two effects at work that cancel each other.

The first effect is when you're playing to win. This attitude improves your performance. The second effect is when you're playing not to lose – it leads to decreased performance.

In their book *Top Dog: The Science of Winning and Losing*[xxiii], Ashley Merryman and Po Bronson show how this effect works in the real world. When professional soccer players were making penalty shots to save their team from losing, they succeeded 62% of the time. When they were making the shots to make their team win, they succeeded 92% of the time.

Consequently, the key to successfully using competitiveness to achieve more is to focus on winning, and not just trying not to be left behind.

When you look at some of the most successful people on the planet, like Richard Branson or Jeff Bezos, it's clear to see that all of them have the mentality of a winner.

Richard Branson always mentions that he never enters an industry unless his company can make a huge difference. In his own words, "Virgin only enters an industry when we think we can offer consumers something strikingly different that will disrupt the market.[xxiv]"

Note the use of the word "disrupt." He's not after merely keeping up with the competition – he wants to transform the entire industry. His often-praised Virgin Atlantic airlines are the perfect example of playing to win.

Jeff Bezos built Amazon to such a huge company because he focused on making it customer-centric. And as he said, "If you're competitor-focused, you have to wait until there is a competitor doing something. Being customer-focused allows you to be more pioneering.[xxv]"

Yet again, it's a perfect example of playing to win. By putting focus on your customer, you constantly raise your standards and innovate instead of merely following the competition so you don't lose.

Playing not to lose is usually characterized by following the trends and playing it safe, while playing to win is about innovation and taking risks. When setting your own goals, do you play to win or play not to lose? If it's the latter, find a way to transform it in the former.

Collaborate When Possible

Studies show that collaboration significantly boosts achievement, motivation, productivity, and the ability to handle challenges[xxvi].

If you struggle with getting enough motivation to start working on a big goal, consider looking for other people who might share your ambitions. It will inspire you to act as well as increase your chances of success.

If you're working on a business, a local co-working space can be a good place to find potential partners or a whole team of people dedicated to achieving the same, big goal. Even if it's just a short conversation by the coffee machine, it can be enough to defeat procrastination.

Richard Branson stresses that no big business-related ideas can succeed without the right team. In his own words, "I learned that the most successful entrepreneurs are those who find people who are at least as good as, or better than, they are at running their businesses[xxvii]."

People – and the effect they have on each other – are the core of the Virgin brand, and that's one of the reasons why the various Virgin companies are so successful.

If you want to transform your body, consider finding a workout buddy/buddies. Due to the Köhler effect, we try harder when we're a part of the group and don't want to be the weakest link.

Studies show[xxviii] that working out with a partner increases performance across multiple sessions. In other words, your chances of reaching a big fitness goal are much higher if you complete each workout with a person who exercises with you.

This effect will also work in other areas of your life. Whenever you can surround yourself with a group of people who will keep you accountable, you'll be much more likely to achieve better results and stick to your goals.

Think Bigger by Surrounding Yourself with the Right People

Social modeling is a fundamental concept of social learning theory that shows how people learn and adapt new behaviors by observation only[xxix]. I already briefly mentioned this topic in the first chapter.

Studies show that we learn from people we observe directly, from instructions given by these people, and by means of media.

It's possible to create social change with soap operas[xxx] because people model the characters they see on the screen. You would say it's such a small influence it shouldn't have any effect on you, yet it works (even if you're not aware of it).

Watching violent television, movies, listening to violent music and playing violent video games increases aggression[xxxi]. Again – sounds like an innocent way to entertain yourself, while in fact it messes up your brain.

In one study, children watching adults behaving aggressively toward a doll were more likely to be aggressive, while children watching adults behaving kindly toward a doll were more likely to be kind, too[xxxii]. Adults aren't that different from kids. Surround yourself with aggressive people, and you'll be aggressive, too.

We acquire both empowering and negative beliefs, behaviors, and opinions of people around us – including those we only see in television, movies, or read about in books. The famous quote by Jim Rohn, "You are the average of the five people you spend the most time with" turns out to be true.

If you want to get more driven and strive for more achievement in your life, surround yourself with highly passionate and ambitious individuals. According to the social learning theory, you can do it in three ways:

1. Live model – watching a person demonstrate a behavior. This means spending time in environments where you can naturally watch other people achieve success. For instance, if you want to become a world-class golf player, you'd find golf courses where you can watch most successful players play.

2. Verbal instruction – listening to an individual describing how to do something. This means making friends with successful, driven people, attending seminars, and/or finding a mentor or a coach.

3. Symbolic – by watching movies, television, browsing the Internet, reading, and listening to podcasts. There are endless sources of materials for success-oriented people. My first recommendation is books. I also like to find a quiet place somewhere outside and listen to audio interviews with successful people.

Eliminate the Negative Influence

Studies show that bad is stronger than good[xxxiii] – we're wired to focus more on the negative information than the positive. Consequently, the negative influence of other people and demotivating media does more harm to your motivation than surrounding yourself with successful individuals.

We already established in the first chapter that mass media thrives on doom and gloom, and isn't conducive to your success.

Watching less news (or ideally, not watching it at all) will reduce your anxiety levels and change your world view. In the world of mass media, only bad things happen in the world. Why strive for more if the world is such a bad place? It's just one of many limiting beliefs mass media puts in your brain.

Whiners and bitter people who might be your colleagues, friends, or family members are another source of negative energy that can affect your mindset. How are you supposed to work with burning motivation on the big things if your relatives or friends constantly poke fun at your ambitious goals?

If there's one thing that is shared by every successful person, it is that they all hang out with other successful people. For a good reason – once you start thinking big, people who haven't grown with you won't be able to relate to you. It's a price you need to pay for achievement – some relationships will weaken, while some will end.

COMPETITIVENESS AND COLLABORATION DRIVE AMBITION: QUICK RECAP

1. Playing to win improves your performance, while playing not to lose affects it negatively. Competition can help you grow as a person only if you concentrate on being the best, and not just catching up to others.

2. Collaboration leads to improved motivation and performance. Whenever possible, find other people who share your big ambitions and work with them.

3. Surround yourself with the right ambitious and driven people. We learn by observation, and the behaviors and beliefs you'll observe in these people will directly affect yours.

4. Everything that surrounds you can have an influence on you. Just like you wouldn't like to spend time around a smoker if you don't smoke, so you shouldn't spend time with people who spread a negative aura around them, as it will poison your well-being just like cigarette smoke.

5. Humans focus more on the bad than the good. Pay special attention to avoiding the negative input coming from others and from mass media. We generally underestimate how detrimental these things can be to our mental health.

Chapter 5: The Art of Focus

Big goals can only be achieved with sustained concentration and focus on the most important aspects. All of the unessential things should be set aside because they take up valuable time without contributing much to the end result.

Jeff Bezos once said, "We've had three big ideas at Amazon that we've stuck with for 18 years, and they're the reason we're successful: Put the customer first. Invent. And be patient.[xxxiv]"

While there are surely much more than just three reasons why Amazon became so successful, there's no arguing that it's Bezos' focus on the essence that made him so successful.

You need to learn how to focus for three reasons:

1. To motivate yourself to work on your big goal. If you don't break it down into smaller parts which affect the outcome the most, it might sound impossible to achieve.

2. To improve your performance. The 80/20 rule applies to every single area of life. Most of the output will always be produced by just a few key factors.

3. To accomplish your task instead of straying off the path. If you don't know how to focus, distractions will lead you in a different direction you might not necessarily want to take.

How do you focus and ensure big results with as little effort as possible? Let's start with the right approach to productivity.

Strategic Laziness

Richard Koch, one of the most successful British entrepreneurs and investors, and bestselling author of books about the 80/20 rule (most notably *The 80/20 Principle: The Secret of Achieving More with Less*[xxxv]) credits much of his success to religiously following the philosophy of doing as little work as possible.

As he explains in his book *Living the 80/20 Way*, "Make a great mental leap: dissociate effort from reward. Focus on the outcomes that you want and find the easiest way to them with least effort, least sacrifice, and most pleasure. Concentrate on what produces extraordinary results without extraordinary effort. Be efficient but relaxed. First, think results. Then get them with least energy.[xxxvi]"

Tim Ferriss, bestselling author and successful angel investor, shares Koch's sentiments by writing in his book *The 4-Hour Workweek*[xxxvii], "Slow down and remember this: Most things make no difference. Being busy is a form of mental laziness-lazy thinking and indiscriminate action."

Focused thinking is even more important when working on the big goals. If you want to achieve them, you can't afford to spend your mental energy and time thinking about the little details that have little to no impact. The more you simplify the goal you want to achieve, the easier and faster you'll achieve it.

Strategic laziness is simple: you focus exclusively on the actions that provide the best results and disregard everything else. The main challenge is to resist the temptation to do more. If you're hyperactive and can't just reduce the amount of hours worked, spend the additional hours working on an entirely different goal.

I set a goal to become a bestselling author with my first book *How to Build Self-Discipline: Resist Temptations and Reach Your Long-Term Goals*. When you research what some people believe is needed to make your book sell well, you'll surely become overwhelmed.

However, when you dig deeper and focus on the most important aspects of writing a book and marketing it, it becomes simple. I disregarded all the little details like starting a blog, releasing press releases, being active on social media, and so on. Instead, I put focus on doing my best when writing the book and picking just a couple of marketing techniques to focus on.

Two weeks after I published this book, it reached #1 in two big categories and appeared on the list of Hot New Releases along with other bestselling books. I've achieved this goal precisely because I chose to ignore all the little details that would only take away my time and energy from what works best.

It's a lazy person's approach, but it's smart laziness. I didn't have to work twelve hours every single day to have a successful book launch. I had plenty of time to recharge my creative energy and put it into writing my next book. The alternative was certain burnout with either similar or worse effects.

Exponential Results

In his book *Bold: How to Go Big, Create Wealth and Impact the World*,[xxxviii] Peter Diamandis explains how exponential results are the driving force behind every single big achievement.

One of the greatest examples is Moore's Law, which states that every twelve to twenty-four months the number of integrated circuits on a transistor doubles. As Diamandis points out, "The smartphone in your pocket is a thousand times faster and million times cheaper than a supercomputer from the 1970s."

If you want to achieve big goals quickly, you need to start thinking in terms of exponential growth rather than linear growth.

Linear growth is when 1 becomes 2, which becomes 3, which becomes 4, and so on.

Exponential growth is when 1 becomes 2, which becomes 4, which becomes 8, and so forth.

If you take 20 linear steps, you'll walk about 30 meters or yards. If you take 20 exponential steps, you'll be approximately 524 kilometers or 325 miles away.

The key to exponential growth is replication – by technology and other people. Obviously you can't apply this approach to personal changes – you can't lose weight or learn a language exponentially – but it's useful to remember it when building your business or other organization.

Exponential growth is a perfect example of applying focus to your goals. Instead of starting right away and performing slow, menial jobs, you find a way to perform the same job faster and with less effort.

Think More, Act Less

In his bestselling book *Essentialism: The Disciplined Pursuit of Less*, Greg McKeown writes, "To discern what is truly essential we need space to think, time to look and listen, permission to play, wisdom to sleep, and the discipline to apply highly selective criteria to the choices we make.[xxxix]"

The process of exploring and comparing different ways of accomplishing your goals effectively is more important than the action itself. In today's fast-moving world, many people believe that if you're busy, you're important. But how often do we stop and ask ourselves if what we're doing is even worth doing?

The whole purpose of setting big goals is to grow as a person. In order to grow, you need to get results. Never mistake motion for action. A rocking horse moves, but I've yet to see a kid who has traveled anywhere on it.

Make it your regular habit to go outside (ideally somewhere in nature, away from other people) and spend an hour or so with your thoughts alone. By putting some distance between you and the rapid-moving world, you'll be able to focus more on the big picture and less on the small details that don't matter.

The vast majority of my most useful insights came from the periods of time when I was relaxed and wasn't even consciously thinking about how to achieve my goals. When your mind relaxes, your subconscious somehow gives you the right answer.

Once, I struggled to find the topic for my next book. Instead of spending hours brainstorming new ideas, I decided to relax a little and let my creativity work behind the scenes. One day, I woke up in the middle of the night and came up with the perfect idea for my next book. My brain worked while I was asleep. I found the solution to my problem with almost no effort.

That's the exact same kind of help you need to solve the problems that will lead you to big achievements.

Get in the Zone

In positive psychology, flow[xl] is the mental state in which you're fully immersed in the process. It's the state of perfect focus, when you concentrate on nothing but the activity you perform. According to psychologist Mihály Csíkszentmihályi, there are three important conditions for the state of flow to occur[xli]:

1. The activity you perform must have a clear goal. Without knowing the direction you're going, you won't achieve flow.

2. You must receive clear and immediate feedback. If you can't judge your performance, you won't be able to maintain the state of flow.

3. You must be confident in your abilities to complete the task you're performing. The perceived difficulty of the task can't be much high than your perceived skills.

These three things are the key to increasing your focus while working on your goals. Flow can be most easily applied to education – for instance, when you're learning a foreign language, and sports – achieving fitness-related goals.

Steven Kotler, author of *The Rise of Superman: Decoding the Science of Ultimate Human Performance,* says that taking risks drives focus into the now and helps achieve the state of flow[xlii]. Pushing your limits by thinking bigger leads to increased focus, which in turn leads to better performance.

Striving to achieve the biggest goals possible – usually by following the approach of "fail fast or fail forward" – will help you increase your focus and achieve results more quickly.

Another trigger of flow is novelty and unpredictability. Automated behaviors won't get you in the state of flow. For this reason, find ways to bring more variety and novelty to what you're doing.

If you're learning a new language, cramming a list of verbs every single day won't get you in the state of flow, while a challenging conversation with a native speaker will.

Driving your car to work is a largely automated behavior. Driving a race car on a demanding race track is how you get into the flow.

Kotler also adds that engaging all your senses in the task at hand is another condition to get into the state of deep flow. It's easiest to engage all the senses in sports where the situation requires you to be aware of everything around you.

In other areas of life, developing more self-awareness by meditation can help you learn how to get more aware of different sensory sources around you.

Psychologist Owen Schaffer adds one more condition to achieve flow: freedom from distractions[xliii]. Block the world around you as much as you can while performing your task – silence your phone, close the door of your room, and clear your schedule so you won't think about the incoming obligation.

THE ART OF FOCUS: QUICK RECAP

1. Strategic laziness is vital to help you achieve your goals more quickly and with less effort. By disassociating effort from reward, you'll produce more results with less sacrifice (that would eventually negatively affect other areas of your life).

2. Putting focus on exponential growth can take you from zero to a huge accomplishment much more quickly than you believe. When working on goals in which you can replicate yourself (by using technology or other people), spend more time thinking how to achieve exponential results rather than following the traditional mindset of linear growth.

3. Never mistake motion for action. People who are busy don't get better results than people who work less, and they're usually depleted of energy.

4. Make it a regular habit to take a break and look at your problems from distance. Spending time in nature, away from everyone else, is conducive to introspection.

5. Flow is a state of mind in which you have perfect focus on the task at hand. In order to achieve the state of flow, you need to have a clear goal, get instant feedback, and be challenged, but not so much that you start doubting in your abilities.

6. Taking risks and pushing your limits is another trigger to get in the zone. Don't be afraid to try things that are likely to result in a failure. Your perception of them (and the likelihood of achieving them) will change once you enter the state of flow.

7. Novelty and variety help you achieve flow, while automation and boredom will decrease your focus. Find ways to make your routine more unpredictable to increase the chance of getting into the zone.

8. Flow is easier to achieve when you engage all the senses on the task at hand. If you struggle with paying attention to different stimuli around you, consider practicing meditation to increase your self-awareness.

9. Freedom from distractions will help you achieve a deeper state of flow. Make your surroundings as distraction-free as possible.

Chapter 6: How to Achieve the Impossible

"Nothing is impossible for a man who refuses to listen to reason" was one of the favorite sayings of a legendary copywriter Gary Halbert. It's one of the truths that guides my life, and perfectly explains how to achieve the impossible.

When you read the history behind some of the biggest achievements in human history, you'll quickly notice how many of them were considered impossible.

Even today, when you consider how much the world has changed since the last century, it sounds impossible. You have access to all of the world's knowledge in your smartphone. You can get to virtually anywhere in the world in a day or two. People live longer and in much better health than ever before.

How much of this vision would come true if the people who are behind it listened to reason? Would we fly planes today? Would there be cars everywhere? Would so many people work from the comfort of their homes, conducting transactions with people from the other side of the world?

If you want to think bigger and be extraordinary, you're bound to hear from other people to get real. It's also likely you'll hear it from yourself – the limits of other people will affect your thinking.

People told me that fasting every single day is unhealthy. Yet, I'm healthier and fitter than ever (note: I don't claim intermittent fasting is for everyone; it just works for me). I believed that I would never deal with my shyness. Yet, today I'm an extremely confident person. People say that you can't learn a foreign language in a few months. Yet, I was easily able to get by in Spanish after just a couple of months of studying.

The Secret of Achieving Ambitious Goals

The secret to achieving bigger and bigger goals is self-efficacy – the strength of the confidence in your abilities. The more you believe you can achieve big things, the easier it will be to achieve the impossible.

Without delving too deep into the concept of self-efficacy (I wrote a book about it – *Confidence: How to Overcome Your Limiting Beliefs and Achieve Your Goals*), there are three things you need to know about it.

First and foremost, the most effective way to develop your self-efficacy is through achieving small wins and persisting in face of obstacles[xliv].

You can't exactly start with nothing and build a billion-dollar business right away, or become a professional bodybuilder after a week of exercising. It takes blood, sweat and tears to get to this point – even when you disassociate effort from reward, challenges still await you.

Secondly, another effective way to develop more confidence in your skills is to watch others achieve success and model your behavior after them. We already covered how to do it. You're much more likely to think bigger and achieve big things if you're surrounded by people who strive to grow every single day.

Last but not least, although self-efficacy is task-related (meaning that confidence in your ability to build a business doesn't directly translate to confidence in your skills to lose weight), your past performance affects all areas of your life. The more success you achieve in one thing, the easier it will be to achieve it in other areas.

For instance, the catalyst for all changes in my life was working out and overcoming my shyness. Making my body stronger and becoming a self-confident person increased my confidence in the general ability to achieve success. It translated into success when learning foreign languages, building a business, and learning other skills like writing.

Self-efficacy is the starting point for all achievements in your life. Without the belief that you can achieve a certain goal, you'll subconsciously sabotage yourself, either by putting too little effort or not even planning how to reach your objectives.

I strongly suggest learning how to overcome your limiting thoughts and gain more confidence in your skills. Bold thinking requires bold attitude, and you won't exhibit it until you learn how to believe in yourself.

It's All about Your Track Record

All successful people started with small things and then turned them into bigger and bigger things. If you have big goals but lack experience, don't just wait until you magically gain it.

Many people wish to start a business, but they constantly postpone their decision while looking for a perfect business idea that will make them millions. That's not how entrepreneurship works. Anything – including selling things on eBay or opening your lemonade stand – is better than inaction and looking for the perfect idea.

Richard Branson started with breeding budgerigars (small parrots) and growing and selling Christmas trees[xlv]. Both businesses failed, but the experience he gained from these ventures helped him later on.

A lot of people would like to write a novel. However, they never get around to it because they believe they need a brilliant idea and incredible writing skills. Guess what... There's no author in the world whose first work was good. Writing takes practice, and the best course of action for most novice writers is to start with short stories and slowly progress to novellas and then novels. Once again, waiting is detrimental to your success.

It's the same with every achievement. If you want to lose weight, you don't need to wait until you're fit enough to run for a mile or longer. You start with short walks, gradually increase the speed and move on to jogging. It's hard to find an obese person who believes she can lose all excess weight – until she focuses on the process and gradually increases her confidence.

Moving from one small thing to a bigger one builds your self-efficacy, while also helping you gain experience and push your limits further and further. Establish your track record, no matter how small your current achievements will be. Bold goals will come later.

A Simple Principle to Shift Big Goals from "Someday" to "Now"

Peter Thiel, cofounder of PayPal, asks in his podcast on Tim Ferriss' show[xlvi] a fascinating question that can shift your mindset: "If you have a 10 year plan and know how to get there, you have to ask: why can't you do this in 6 months?"

Often we move our big goals to somewhere in the future, thinking that we're not ready yet. And although sometimes it's a valid approach (you can't become a surgeon in 6 months), in many instances it's possible to shorten the waiting period or start right away.

Let's say you want to learn a foreign language someday when you'll have more free time. But let's be honest with yourself –you really can't find at least 15 minutes a day to learn it? Even 15 minutes a day is better than nothing. It's almost two hours of studying a week. Instead of achieving this goal *someday* (either never or at least a few years from now), you can achieve it in a year or two.

Another example: you'd like to build a business, but in your plan it can't happen sooner than in two years because you want to save enough money to quit your job and start it then. But in life, there are rarely just two choices. It's not about quitting your job or starting your business. You can build your business on the side, and keep your job until your business gains enough traction to warrant giving in your notice.

Often the only reason why we postpone acting on our goals is a lack of confidence in our abilities. The only solution to this problem is to start – self-efficacy won't build itself. The impossible is possible, but only if you start.

Shorter Deadlines Lead to Better Results

It's an old adage that the amount of time one has to perform a task is the amount of time it will take to complete the task. The shorter your deadlines are, the more pressured you are to come up with a better way to achieve your goal. The longer your deadlines are, the more likely you are to procrastinate and take the less effective, manual approach.

One example where this law is visible is writing books. Many people have a dream to write a book. Some of them act on it and work on their novel every now and then with no clear deadline. The most common outcome is that they will never finish writing it.

Now consider what would happen if they set a goal to finish it in three months. Three months is a lot of time, but it's short enough to increase your focus instead of dilly dallying. Stephen King, arguably one of the best fiction writers, finishes the first draft of his novel in three months[xlvii]. If he can do it – and write a bestselling story – so can you (perhaps without the bestselling part – at least not if it's your first story).

I like to impose short deadlines on myself, as they increase my concentration, help me focus on the essence, and achieve my goals much sooner.

Without the pressure to act quickly, it would take me many more years to learn how to write books. However, since for several months I wrote about 100,000 words per month, I paid my dues much sooner than writers who set long deadlines and need a year, if not longer, to write their first 100,000 words (while, with a short deadline, you could already reach a million written words).

HOW TO ACHIEVE THE IMPOSSIBLE: QUICK RECAP

1. Nothing is impossible for a man who refuses to listen to reason. If you set big goals, people will tell you you're unreasonable. But they've told many successful inventors and other people who have changed the world.

2. You need to believe in your abilities to achieve success. There are three important things you need to know about self-efficacy: you build it by achieving small wins and persisting in the face of setbacks; modeling after others can help you increase your confidence; your past successes will improve your general confidence and help you achieve other goals.

3. Nobody has achieved big goals right away. You start with small achievements and gradually increase the level of your success. Waiting will only lead to inaction and wasted time.

4. Ask yourself how you can achieve your 10-year plan in 6 months or less. Oftentimes we postpone our goals simply because we make excuses or don't think creatively.

5. Set short deadlines to achieve much more in much less time. One of the reasons why people never complete their goals is a lack of urgency. By setting short deadlines (and sticking to them), you'll get ahead, while others will still be taking their first steps.

Chapter 7: The Dangers of Being Overly Ambitious (and How to Avoid Them)

While thinking bigger and trying to set the bar higher and higher is an admirable quality, being an overachiever can put a lot of pressure on you. Increased stress will affect both your mental and physical health, which will in turn lead to deteriorated performance and burnout.

Consequently, in the last chapter of this book, we'll cover some ways you can find the right balance between achievement and recharging.

The Art of Balance

Achieving perfect work-life balance is a popular myth that, unfortunately, applies to nobody. Your professional life will affect your personal life, and your personal life will affect your professional life.

However, while it's impossible not to take your job with you after work (and it's even more difficult if you're an entrepreneur), there are ways to reduce time spent thinking about work while you're supposed to relax.

The first key to recharge more while relaxing is to enter the state of flow. Flow can happen while working on a goal, but you can also get in the zone while relaxing. Various sports, and most notably extreme sports and any other activities with perceived high risk and challenge, are perfect to get your mind off work.

The second way to achieve more balance is to spend more time in nature. Studies show[xlviii] that physical activity in a forest or a park helps recover from stress. I recommend spending at least an hour a week alone, in a quiet place away from everyone else. If you can't take your mind off work, consider listening to music or taking a book or an e-reader with you.

Gary Keller, co-owner of one of the biggest international real estate franchises, writes in his bestselling book *The One Thing: The Surprisingly Simple Truth Behind Extraordinary Results*[xlix] about three ways people try to achieve balance between work and life.

The first approach is living in the middle – paying equal attention to work and life. This approach won't work for people who want to achieve big things because you can't achieve extraordinary results with a balanced approach. Extraordinary happens at the extremes, and if you only pay moderate attention to your work, you won't achieve big things.

The second approach is going to the extremes – spending a lot of time at work for long periods of time and then trying to fix the damage done to your personal life by ignoring your work. This approach is just as bad as the first approach. While you can achieve big goals with this attitude, everything else in your life will suffer.

In his novel *Suzanne's Diary for Nicholas*, James Patterson provides a powerful metaphor that has stuck with me since I read it for the first time in Keller's book:

"Imagine life is a game in which you are juggling five balls. The balls are called work, family, health, friends, and integrity. And you're keeping all of them in the air. But one day you finally come to understand that work is a rubber ball. If you drop it, it will bounce back. The other four balls… are made of glass. If you drop one of these, it will be irrevocably scuffed, nicked, perhaps even shattered.[1]"

If these two approaches don't work, then what does?

Keller suggests the third approach – counterbalancing. With this approach, you never go long periods of time without paying attention to your personal life. It always gets a similar level of focus. With your work life, you frequently go to the extremes, but only for short periods of time so your personal life won't suffer. This approach requires you to sacrifice the unessential aspects of your work in pursuit of working on the biggest things.

This approach is the healthiest attitude. It will guarantee extraordinary results, while working on your goals while still paying attention to your personal life.

Being Ambitious Doesn't Mean Self-Harm

Going to the extremes with your work doesn't mean working extremely long hours.

Many entrepreneurs brag how little sleep they get and how much they work. It's a shame they often forget they're working on their goals to achieve results, not to show off how well they can function in an exhausted state.

Martyrdom sounds cool, but it won't help you achieve your goals.

A paper by John Pencavel of Stanford University[li] shows that working for more than 50 hours per week leads to decreased productivity, while working for more than 55 hours doesn't produce any additional results. If you have a 70-hour workweek, you essentially waste 15 hours per week.

Sleep deprivation is a silent killer of productivity and your well-being. A week of sleeping four or five hours per night is equal to an impairment equivalent to a blood alcohol level of 1‰[lii] (four to five glasses of beer).

Two weeks of sleeping four to five hours per night makes the symptoms two times worse. Your ability to solve problems dramatically deteriorates, your reaction time greatly lengthens, your judgment is clouded. How do you expect to achieve big things in such a horrible state?

Martyrdom isn't reserved for entrepreneurs only. You can also be tempted to exhibit this behavior if you're working on other big goals.

People who want to transform their bodies think that the more they work out, the stronger and fitter they'll be. Yet, you don't get a flat stomach in the gym – you get it in your kitchen by maintaining the proper diet.

Exercising three times per week for 45 minutes is more than enough to get results[liii], while overtraining is a perfect way to get injured and lose months of progress due to long recovery.

People who want to learn new skills spend countless hours practicing and memorizing new things, thinking that it's the studying time that counts.

In reality, it's the other way around. Your brain needs sleep to learn, not just more practice. Studies show that a nap of 45–60 minutes can boost your memory five-fold[liv].

As neuropsychologist Axel Mecklinger from the research team said, "Even a short nap in the office or a nap at school can improve learning outcomes significantly."

Start with the foundation – proper sleep and enough rest – and only then work on your goals.

THE DANGERS OF BEING OVERLY AMBITIOUS (AND HOW TO AVOID THEM): QUICK RECAP

1. It's essential to learn how to recharge your batteries and get your mind off working on big things. If you don't do it, your performance will deteriorate, and you'll suffer from negative effects of stress. Moreover, your personal life will suffer.

2. You can't achieve perfect balance between work and your personal life. The proper approach is to never go long periods of time without paying attention to your personal life and going to the extremes with your work life. The reason for that is that achievement happens at the extremes, while your personal life is fragile, and dropping it for long periods of time will ruin it.

3. Don't be a martyr. Working longer hours doesn't lead to better performance. Sleep deprivation makes you act like a drunk person. Take care of the fundments before you start working on your goals – unless you enjoy clouded judgment and impaired ability to solve problems.

Epilogue

Tony Robbins frequently says that the key to success is to raise your standards.

By constantly working on improving your life, you'll feel fulfillment, which will give your life a meaning. This, in turn, will lead to happiness and even more achievement.

Thinking bigger is exactly what you need if you'd like to get more driven and passionate about your everyday life.

In the seven chapters of this book, we covered some of the most important aspects of thinking big. Some of the most important lessons from the book include:

1. Surrounding yourself with the right, positive energy is the key to success. Strive to spend time with people who empower you and motivate you to reach bigger and bigger goals. Read books that will inspire you to change your life. Listen to podcasts that will educate you on how to get even better at what you do.

2. Achievement can't happen without proper, powerful intrinsic motivation. If you make your "why" bigger than you and superficial things like money or status, you'll get even more fired up to work on your goals and make big things happen.

3. The primal part of your brain can sabotage you when trying to make changes in your life. The key to managing your chimp is self-awareness and using the routines and rituals to reduce its influence on your behavior.

4. Play to win instead of playing not to lose. There's a huge difference between the mindset of a winner and the mindset of a person who just doesn't want to stay behind. Don't be afraid to follow an unconventional approach to achieve your goals.

5. Laziness is not a bad thing as long as it's strategic. Disassociate effort from reward and focus on achieving results with as little work as possible. The keys are to focus on the most essential things and make your work fun. This ties with your "why" – if you aren't passionate about what you're doing, it will be hard to achieve extraordinary results.

6. Nothing is impossible for a man who refuses to listen to reason. Your beliefs establish your limits. If you stop thinking reasonably and instead ask yourself how you can achieve the impossible, you'll come up with a way to do it.

7. Martyrdom won't lead you to achievement. Pay close attention to your personal life and never sacrifice it to achieve your goals. If you don't heed this advice, don't be surprised that after achieving your goal you won't have anything to go back to.

The research I conducted for this book has made me realize that the key to thinking bigger is changing your mindset. You can learn all the little tricks you want, but if you don't change your mind, achievement won't follow.

Make it a habit to pay close attention to your thoughts and limiting beliefs. This process will help you filter negativity that prevents you from setting bolder goals and believing in yourself.

What big goal are you going to work on now?

Appendix A: Books You Need to Read

As we covered it in the first chapter, books can change your life. They have transformed mine, and they have changed the lives of all the most successful people in the world.

In this appendix, I'll share with you some of my favorite life-changing books that can change your life, too. They are listed in random order except for the first and the last title.

1. MJ DeMarco's *The Millionaire Fastlane: Crack the Code to Wealth and Live Rich for a Lifetime*. Business books of this kind often get a bad rap for vague, purely motivational advice, but every now and then someone writes a legendary book that outshines every other book in this genre. MJ's approach is a perfect example of thinking big. In the book, he teaches you how to become a rich person in a few years instead of several decades. It's a must-

read for every person who wants to build a business and become rich.

2. Books by Richard Branson – including *Losing My Virginity*, *Screw It, Let's Do It*, Like a *Virgin: Secrets They Won't Teach You at Business School*, and *The Virgin Way: How to Listen, Learn, Laugh and Lead*. There are few people in the world who think bigger than Richard Branson. His entire persona is the embodiment of bold thinking. Dive into his mind by reading his books and change your life.

3. Peter Diamandis' *Abundance: The Future Is Better Than You Think* and *Bold: How to Go Big, Create Wealth and Impact the World*. The first book will help you develop the abundant mindset by realizing how much our world has changed and how much better the future is going to be. The second book is the guide to thinking big and changing the world. If you want to join the likes of Elon Musk, Jeff Bezos and Richard Branson, you need to read it.

4. Richard Koch's books about the 80/20 principle like *The 80/20 Principle: The Secret of Achieving More with Less*, *Living the 80/20 Way* or

The 80/20 Individual. Richard Koch is the perfect example of how to achieve more with less. He's one of the wealthiest Britons. His investments (guided by simple principles) have made him extraordinary returns. If you want to learn how to achieve more with less, read everything written by this brilliant mind.

5. Greg McKeown's *Essentialism: The Disciplined Pursuit of Less*. If you want to explore more about how to focus and simplify your life, this book is for you. You can't achieve big things if you concern yourself with things that don't matter much. Greg will teach you how to identify and disregard these things.

6. Gary Keller's *The One Thing: The Surprisingly Simple Truth Behind Extraordinary Results*. The title alone perfectly explains what this book is about. If you want to achieve incredible results in a short time frame, you'll learn how to do it in Gary's book. His advice can be also applied to improving your personal life.

7. Peter Thiel's *Zero to One: Notes on Startups, or How to Build the Future*. A must-read for everyone who wants to build an innovative business. Peter is the perfect example of bold thinking, having created PayPal and investing in some of the world's most influential startups like Facebook.

8. Tim Ferriss' books *The 4-Hour Workweek*, *The 4-Hour Body*, and *The 4-Hour Chef*. All three books will help you optimize your life.

The 4-Hour Workweek will show you how to escape your day job and start a lifestyle business. But don't stop there – use the money made from your lifestyle business to go even bigger.

The 4-Hour Body will show you how to achieve big fitness goals. If you want to transform your body or become a world-class athlete, this book is for you. Tim's tips (among others) helped me lose 30 pounds in three months.

The 4-Hour Chef will show you how to master new skills by putting focus on the most essential things. The principles from this book will help you become a world-class expert.

9. Jay Abraham's books *Getting Everything You Can Out of All You've Got: 21 Ways You Can Out-Think, Out-Perform, and Out-Earn the Competition* and *The Sticking Point Solution: 9 Ways to Move Your Business from Stagnation to Stunning Growth in Tough Economic Times*. If you want to build a big business that makes a real difference to your clients, reading everything by Jay Abraham is a must.

10. Tony Robbins' classics *Unlimited Power* and *Awaken the Giant Within*. Tony Robbins is arguably the most knowledgeable life coach in the world. His insights about human psychology can dramatically shift your mindset. If I were to choose two of the most transformative books I've ever read, I would pick these two exceptional titles.

Download another Book for Free

I want to thank you for buying my book and offer you another book (just as long and valuable as this book), *Grit: How to Keep Going When You Want to Give Up*, completely free.

Click the link below to receive it:

http://www.profoundselfimprovement.com/thinkbigger

In *Grit*, I'll share with you how exactly to stick to your goals according to peak performers and science.

In addition to getting *Grit*, you'll also have an opportunity to get my new books for free, enter giveaways and receive other valuable emails from me.

Again, here's the link to sign up:

http://www.profoundselfimprovement.com/thinkbigger

Could You Help?

I'd love to hear your opinion about my book. In the world of book publishing, there are few things more valuable than honest reviews from a wide variety of readers.

Your review will help other readers find out whether my book is for them. It will also help me reach more readers by increasing the visibility of my book.

About Martin Meadows

Martin Meadows is the pen name of an author who has dedicated his life to personal growth. He constantly reinvents himself by making drastic changes in his life.

Over the years, he has regularly fasted for over 40 hours, taught himself two foreign languages, lost over 30 pounds in 12 weeks, ran several businesses in various industries, took ice-cold showers and baths, lived on a small tropical island in a foreign country for several months, and wrote a 400-page long novel's worth of short stories in one month.

Yet, self-torture is not his passion. Martin likes to test his boundaries to discover how far his comfort zone goes.

His findings (based both on his personal experience and scientific studies) help him improve his life. If you're interested in pushing your limits and learning how to become the best version of yourself, you'll love Martin's works.

You can read his books here:

http://www.amazon.com/author/martinmeadows.

© Copyright 2015 by Meadows Publishing. All rights reserved.

Reproduction in whole or in part of this publication without express written consent is strictly prohibited. The author greatly appreciates you taking the time to read his work. Please consider leaving a review wherever you bought the book, or telling your friends about it, to help us spread the word. Thank you for supporting our work.

Efforts have been made to ensure that the information in this book is accurate and complete. However, the author and the publisher do not warrant the accuracy of the information, text and graphics contained within the book due to the rapidly changing nature of science, research, known and unknown facts and the Internet. The author and the publisher do not hold any responsibility for errors, omissions or contrary interpretation of the subject matter herein. This book is presented solely for motivational and informational purposes only.

References

[i] http://content.time.com/time/magazine/article/0,9171,1126746-1,00.html, Web. March 21st, 2015.

[ii] Bandura A. (1963). *Social learning and personality development*. New York: Holt, Rinehart, and Winston.

[iii] Dobelli R., "Avoid News: Towards a Healthy News Diet", www.dobelli.com, 2010.

[iv] Listen to Tim Ferriss' interview with Peter Diamandis and Tony Robbins by visiting this link: http://fourhourworkweek.com/2014/10/07/global-learning-xprize/

[v] Brown I., Inouye D. K. "Learned helplessness through modeling: The role of perceived similarity in competence." *Journal of Personality and Social Psychology* 1978, 36 (8): 900–908. See also: Bandura, A. (1981). *Self-referent thought: A development analysis of self-efficacy*. In J. H. Flavell & L. Ross (Eds.), *Social cognitive development: Frontiers and possible futures* (pp. 200–239). Cambridge, England: Cambridge University Press.

[vi] Baumeister R.F., Bratslavsky E., Finkenauer C., Vohs K. D. "Bad is stronger than good." *Review of General Psychology* 2001; 5: 323–370.

[vii] http://liveyourlegend.net/productivity-guide-how-richard-branson-does-so-much-the-power-of-fitness/, Web. March 21st, 2015.

[viii] Kahneman D., Deaton A. "High income improves evaluation of life but not emotional well-being." *Proceedings of the National Academy of Sciences of the United States of America* 2010; 107 (38): 16489–16493.

[ix] Cho Y. J., Perry J. L. "Intrinsic Motivation and Employee Attitudes: Role of Managerial Trustworthiness, Goal Directedness, and Extrinsic Reward Expectancy." *Review of Public Personnel Administration* 2012; 32 (4): 382–406.

[x] Gagné M., Deci E. L. "Self-determination theory and work motivation." *Journal of Organizational Behavior* 2005; 26 (4): 331–362.

[xi] Srivastava A., Locke E. A., Bartol K. M. "Money and subjective well-being: it's not the money, it's the motives." *Journal of Personality and Social Psychology* 2001; 80 (6): 959–71.

[xii] http://www.virgin.com/entrepreneur/richard-bransons-top-20-virgin-inspirational-insights, Web. March 23rd, 2015.

[xiii] Grant A. M. "Does Intrinsic Motivation Fuel the Prosocial Fire? Motivational Synergy in Predicting Persistence, Performance, and Productivity." *Journal of Applied Psychology* 2008; 93 (1): 48–58.

[xiv] http://www.businessinsider.com/brilliant-elon-musk-quotes-2014-6?op=1, Web. March 23rd, 2015.

[xv] http://fourhourworkweek.com/2014/10/15/money-master-the-game/, Web. March 22nd, 2015.

[xvi] Pham L. B., Taylor S. E. (1999). "From Thought to Action: Effects of Process-Versus Outcome-Based Mental Simulations on Performance." *Personality and Social Psychology Bulletin* 1999; 25 (2): 250–260.

[xvii] The quote most likely originates from the poem *Thinking* by Walter D. Wintle cited in the beginning of this book.

[xviii] Duhigg C., *The Power of Habit: Why We Do What We Do in Life and Business*.

[xix] Peters S., *The Chimp Paradox: The Mind Management Program to Help You Achieve Success, Confidence, and Happiness*.

[xx] Robbins T., *Unlimited Power: The New Science Of Personal Achievement*.

[xxi] Robbins T., *Awaken the Giant Within: How to Take Immediate Control of Your Mental, Emotional, Physical and Financial Destiny*.

[xxii] Murayama K., Elliot A. J. "The competition–performance relation: a meta-analytic review and test of the opposing

processes model of competition and performance." *Psychological Bulletin* 2012; 138 (6): 1035–1070.

[xxiii] Merryman A., Bronson P., *Top Dog: The Science of Winning and Losing.*

[xxiv] http://www.virgin.com/entrepreneur/five-individuals-who-failed-and-recovered-in-style, Web. March 23rd, 2015.

[xxv] http://www.businessinsider.com/jeff-bezos-amazon-growth-quotes-2014-9?op=1, Web. March 23rd, 2015.

[xxvi] Bandura A. "Exercise of human agency through collective efficacy." *Current Directions in Psychological Science* 2000; 9: 75–78.

[xxvii] http://www.entrepreneur.com/article/219988, Web. March 23rd, 2015.

[xxviii] Irwin B. C., Scorniaenchi J., Kerr N. L., Eisenmann J. C., Feltz D. L. "Aerobic exercise is promoted when individual performance affects the group: a test of the Kohler motivation gain effect." *Annals of Behavioral Medicine* 2012; 44 (2): 151–159.

[xxix] Bandura A. (1963). *Social learning and personality development*. New York: Holt, Rinehart, and Winston.

[xxx] Bandura, A. (2004). "Social cognitive theory for personal and social change by enabling media". In A. Singhal, M. J. Cody, E. M. Rogers, & M. Sabido (Eds.), *Entertainment-education and social change: History, research, and practice* (pp. 75-96). Mahwah, NJ: Lawrence Erlbaum.

[xxxi] Anderson C. A., Berkowitz L., Donnerstein E., Huesmann L. R., Johnson J. D., Linz D., Malamuth N. M., Wartella E. "The influence of media violence on youth." *Psychological Science in the Public Interest* 2003; 4 (3): 81.

[xxxii] Bandura A., Ross D., Ross S. A. "Imitation of film-mediated aggressive models." *The Journal of Abnormal and Social Psychology* 1963; 66 (1): 3–11.

[xxxiii] Baumeister R.F., Bratslavsky E., Finkenauer C., Vohs K. D. "Bad is stronger than good." *Review of General Psychology* 2001; 5: 323–370.

[xxxiv] http://www.businessinsider.com/jeff-bezos-amazon-growth-quotes-2014-9?op=1#ixzz3VCG0A2s0, Web. March 23rd, 2015.

[xxxv] Koch R., *The 80/20 Principle: The Secret of Achieving More with Less.*

[xxxvi] Koch R., *Living the 80/20 Way: Work Less, Worry Less, Succeed More, Enjoy More.*

[xxxvii] Ferriss T., *The 4-Hour Workweek: Escape 9-5, Live Anywhere, and Join the New Rich.*

[xxxviii] Diamandis P. H., Kotler S., *Bold: How to Go Big, Create Wealth and Impact the World.*

[xxxix] Mckeown G., *Essentialism: The Disciplined Pursuit of Less.*

[xl] Mihaly Csikszentmihalyi (1990). *Flow: The Psychology of Optimal Experience.* Harper & Row.

[xli] Csikszentmihalyi M., Abuhamdeh S., Nakamura, J. (2005), "Flow", in Elliot, A., *Handbook of Competence and Motivation*, New York: The Guilford Press, pp. 598–698

[xlii] http://www.fastcompany.com/3031052/the-future-of-work/how-to-hack-into-your-flow-state-and-quintuple-your-productivity, Web. March 24th, 2015.

[xliii] Schaffer O. (2013), *Crafting Fun User Experiences: A Method to Facilitate Flow*, Human Factors International

[xliv] Bandura A. (1997) *Self-efficacy: The exercise of control.* New York: Freeman.

[xlv] http://www.entrepreneur.com/article/225527, Web. March 24th, 2015.

[xlvi] http://fourhourworkweek.com/2014/09/09/peter-thiel/, Web. March 24th, 2015.

[xlvii] King S., *On Writing.*

[xlviii] Hansmann R., Hug S. M., Seeland K. "Restoration and stress relief through physical activities in forests and parks." *Urban Forestry & Urban Greening* 2007; 6 (4): 213–225.

[xlix] Keller G., Papasan J., *The ONE Thing: The Surprisingly Simple Truth Behind Extraordinary Results.*

[l] Patterson J., *Suzanne's Diary for Nicholas.*

[li] Pencavel J. *The Productivity of Working Hours*, Discussion Paper No. 8129, April 2014.

[lii] Fryer B. *Sleep Deficit: The Performance Killer*, *Harvard Business Review*, October 2006.

[liii] For sensible advice on how to work out effectively and safely, read *Beyond Brawn* by Stuart McRobert.

[liv] Studte S., Bridger E., Mecklinger A. "Nap sleep preserves associative but not item memory performance." *Neurobiology of Learning and Memory* 2015, 120: 84–93.

Printed in Great Britain
by Amazon